# A GIRL IS A SHAPESHIFTER
poems by Jasmine S. Higgins

A Girl Is A Shapeshifter
Copyright © 2019 Jasmine S. Higgins
ISBN: 978-1-5272-5197-7

Higgins, Jasmine S.
First edition.

Author photo by Joshua Higgins
Proofread by Toby Dunlop and John Ferrer
Cover design by Jasmine Higgins
Illustrated by Jasmine Higgins

# TABLE OF CONTENTS

## NICE TO MEET YOU

let me write you into all of my beginnings and none
of my ends. i'll take you through buttercup fields and
crystal waters, never to reach the crumbling cliffs;
always at the punchline and never the point where
our inside jokes get old.

let me talk you through the plants on my windowsill.
i'll call them by their names but i won't tell you how
often they need watering. you only need to know the
surface things
the fun bits
the beginnings;
no need to worry about maintenance.

let me tell you about all the wild things i've done,
all the times i've come undone for men just like you,
but let me skim over the parts where they broke my
heart. let's just sit in the sun and never worry when
the horizon swallows it—remember, it'll be back in
the morning. remember, we don't do goodbyes.

let me taste the breeze as it passes your neck; as you
carry me and sing to me and laugh at everything i
say because all the furniture smells new and all the
spines are yet to be cracked. let me hang my hopeful
head over your shoulder with eyes wide open,
watching as we take our first steps away from your
parked car. let me fill with bubbles of pink
champagne and a strong feeling the road ahead that
i can't see is infinite, but never let me turn to face it.
don't let me know how much time we have left.

just keep singing and i'll keep watching as the car disappears into the hovering fog, tracing your name along your back so i don't forget. tracing the words *nice to meet you.*

## THE INVASION

please excuse me
while i set myself on fire
and throw myself
into your son's arms

- *meeting the parents*

## AUGUST

the skies come undone like loose braids
stars scatter like falling glitter
and the sea just watches from its living room
adjusts the rippling blankets
tucks in its toes

the world waited so long for us to meet
you with the half-smiling face that thinks it knows
everything until i tumble down and leave your mouth
lost, unsure where to go
and me with the chlorine hair and the tired eyes,
sad like a drain but heart beating like
water dripping
and eyes forever unravelling you

sand sticks to skin like sweets stick to their wrappers
your fingers dust me clean and turn me to dirt
all at once
tracing freckles on arms until constellations light up

feed me matchsticks until my chest burns bright
like fireflies in tuscany

pull my hairband out and watch the stars trickle
down the back of my neck
keep one hand on my body as you reach up with the
other, tap the waves above our heads,
and tell the ocean,
'you don't wanna miss this.'

## IS THIS A KINK?

your hand rests tenderly on my cheek
and it hurts because someday you'll leave me.

i think i like it like this
breathe me in and cough me up
hold me soft and drop me
open the door for me
and climb out the window

i like how my stomach turns when you don't reply
how i stoop in disappointment when i learn
something i don't like about you

how i giggle like i'm taking over the world when
you give me attention
and i break like sugar glass when you take it away.

i like you and i don't want you to go,
but i want to be scared that you will.
i want you to play the game how i know you're
going to play it anyway
and i want to hate it.

## ART STUDENTS

a boy drags an empty bed frame through the door,
places it on the ground, and jumps onto it— his feet
crashing through its belly, leaving it wounded.

nobody looks up to see where all the noise is coming
from.

one girl stands on a ladder while another hands her
nails. they're hanging a curtain from the ceiling.
behind the curtain is a pile of ash.

someone spilled their coffee in the corner and we all
know it was deliberate.
we enclose it with the police tape our friend was
carrying in her pocket.

our tutor calls out, 'has anyone seen edward?'
sherrie tells her he's gone on a silent retreat with his
boyfriend.
the tutor frowns. 'his attendance is low.'
'yeah but he's doing it for an art project.'
'oh, fine. has anyone got a cigarette?'

two boys contemplate a single brick.
'i don't think we should risk adding anything.'

sherrie paints yellow over yellow and asks the boy in
the broken bed if she should add more yellow.

i don't know if i belong here, but neither does anyone else. i guess there are worse places to be.

the kid who spilled coffee returns. they notice the police tape, frown for a moment, and then they smile.

## LIGHT

the sun is not himself today
but i'll dance for him anyway

*- on loving someone with depression*

## SLEEPWALKING OR TELEPORTING

the blinding moon stares me down like a flashlight
and i don't know what it wants from me

the window lets in a sliver of earth's creeping smells
and the heaviness of the soil gives me dreams of
coffins

branches of trees stand out like daggers in fists
fighting for or against me
i can never tell

toes wrapped deep in gravel and shivering weeds
tell me i don't belong here
i know that

i look back to the moon, still glaring down at me
i'm sorry, i say
i was just hoping for directions

## TELL ME

just touch me
see, you can't resist it, can you?
how does that feel?
do you like my tits?
do you like me?
tell me i'm perfect
tell me you love me
tell me

is it okay that i do this
every time you start to look bored?
every time you're not thinking about me?
is it okay that i panic
and my panic manifests as horny?

is it okay that i only love sex
when i think it can save me?

## BALLOON

so it turns out
you can't fill vacancies in your life
with empty people
and expect to feel whole

*- sorry if i drained you of things you didn't have*

## 2 DEGREES CELSIUS

i am shaking
decaying
in a single bed

this is winter's way
of telling me
it's over.

## A DYING GAME

*"i can feel my heart beginning to break
it's never happened this slow"*

we broke up 8 months after i wrote that.
8 months
we lay together in your coffin
*(it was cramped and hard to breathe)*
because neither of us knew how to say goodbye.
*(now what do we do with all this space?
all this air that doesn't smell like us?)*

we buried our lovers
sunk memories like ships
until we forgot where we came from
but we held hands through it all.
we kissed each other's cheeks
until giggles broke out like the plague
until the empty turned to ache
and the ache felt so much like love.

no, but there was so much love
have you ever watched a dying flame mourn
in the ashes of a house he couldn't bear
to stop touching?

we were a fire that refused to be put out
we were everything that breaks
sometimes i couldn't tell the right kind of pain
from the wrong kind
so, i said, give me all of it
i want to feel everything that you can do to me

maybe that's how i managed to look the other way
while the walls fell down.

maybe our love went too fast
because we went in with teeth bared
and hungry hands
but honey, now that i'm alone,
love has never felt so slow.

sometimes i wish we'd never met.

## PERFORMANCE ARTIST

i get my tits out on camera, and feminists love me
because i've got my tits out, and misogynists love
me because i've got my tits out, but it doesn't make
me feel good.

art is magic
art is freedom
art runs through the earth's veins
fills spaces with reasons to stay alive
and i am so lucky that i get to create
but my god,
art is soul-crushing.

and i tell people this.
i tell people it doesn't make me happy anymore
that being naked on camera doesn't feel brave,
empowering, necessary, it just feels stupid
and all anyone has to say is,
'that's so powerful.
the way you resent the art,
it really
adds to the art.'

and i know i have nothing
no proof i have a single skill
that isn't creative
i know i have absolutely nothing else to turn to
but i really fucking wish someone would say,

'so just quit.
you're allowed to quit.'

## THE MYTH

you think you know it but you don't.
you can recognise a change in her face,
in the sounds, muscles tensing
no. you've never seen it.
you think you saw it in porn
where you learnt to fuck me the way i don't want
you to, where i learnt to fake it
so many men who've touched my soul
not once saw it leave my body

you know how to touch me
how to turn me into a human waterfall
begging for more, m o r e
that means it's not enough
how can you say that you love me
when you've never seen me leave the ground

sometimes you make me feel something
and i tell myself maybe it is enough
maybe i don't need the
i-think-i-might-be-dying-but-i-don't-mind
rush that i have from time to time
the feeling where i might as well
be living my whole life all at once
condensed into a momentary earthquake

but no, it is not enough
i should not have to beg for more
of something you never gave me.

*- i've seen myself fly and you're missing out*

## RAGDOLL

when you texted me a breakdown and a half,
i was fine.
i was doing great, actually
and you said i could tell you to leave,
i could tell you i didn't wanna talk
and that i've moved on.

but i have this shouting need
to just stop being okay
whenever you aren't.
i'll let you ruin my day
so that you won't feel alone
in the suffering
in the pain
(which i already went through, but hey
i can handle being dragged back and forth
and getting scratched up on the way
as long as it's for you).

i would die by your side
to avoid letting you think
that i was stronger
that i didn't care as much
that my love wasn't as big as yours.

you tell me
post-breakdown
that you need to focus on yourself.
yeah.
me too.

## THE ONE

don't mind me, i'm just waiting
for a knight in shining armour
to come along and shoot me dead

# THE INTERNET IS A SEX PARADE

i browse through the app
acting as if i know what the hell i'm looking for
fingers flicker left and right, sentencing men to death
putting few aside for further consideration

'wanna be jasMINE?;)' one of them asks as his
opening message
a demonstration of how fucking clever he is

another says 'we can only go further if my dog likes
you'
and pictures prove that his dog
lives with his parents
and any guy who wants to introduce a girl to his
parents before getting to know her himself
probably still sucks his thumb

a third guy eloquently asks 'alright darlin x'
and he's the one who catches my eye because he's
not even trying
(this is an unhealthy thing to look for,
and i'll realise that later when i'm crying
and he tells me to let him know when i'm
finished because he 'can't be dealing
with that')
his accent makes me melt into syrup
and he splashes me all over the room
and this is the crime scene i was looking for

when i finally send him away
back into the pile of potentials
ready to be picked up by another girl
i'll look for someone different, someone who cares
and before i know it, i'll be back to a guy who cares
too much

who can't let me out of his sight
can't bear to let anyone else talk
because he's troubled
and he needs to tell everyone who he is
before they start guessing and figure him out

i've already had one of those
that's what the careless man
is here to make up for
and when the careless man is gone
i'll need another catastrophe
to make me forget him

love is a repeat pattern
and i will never learn

## WAR

love isn't dead
but it will be when i'm finished with it

## UNNATURAL DISASTER

the house is mad at me.
i asked the window for some light
and it rolled over so i couldn't see its face
the way my ex did
the night before he sent me away.

i sat in the dark, tried to meditate,
ordered sweet potato fries instead
glared at the bicycle symbol
on the delivery app
moving closer and further
unable to find my house

this happens a lot
but this time it's because the house has swallowed
me up and disappeared
leaving a hole in the town nearly big enough to bury
my mistakes in
a gaping mess where a delivery man is stood,
unsure what to do
tapping at the map sighing 'this can't be right'

the house told me i don't deserve to be here
and i know it's true
i ask where it's taking me and it doesn't respond
i press my phone screen against my eyes
wide open, filling with bloody cracks
soaking up the last light i'll ever see

i think i've totally lost it

## SPILLING

i empty my heart out to you
and by the time i am finished,
the bed is littered with old card receipts
expired lipsticks
3 half-finished bottles of hand sanitiser
a stale biscuit
and a crisp packet from 1997

the clear-out was a little overdue, i admit
the way i've tidied every time you come over is
i've chucked everything in the closet
lit candles to suffocate the sour in the air
stuffed headaches under the bed
along with every heartbreak i've never addressed
and at this point, it's all gotten a little heavy

i can't tell you how much better it feels
now that i've told you the truth
scraped old gum from all the furniture
pulled dead mice from beneath the carpet
i ask you if you're okay
and you say yes,
picking crumbs and decay off your skin

you always wanted me to open up
but look
this is what honesty has done to us
now you can see it, there's just far too much of me
and my whole bedroom makes you itch.

## DEALMAKER

he doesn't listen to a word i say
my god, it's so manly

## GIRLS

why is it that even at my most confident
i write about other girls as if they're
bohemian doves with dior lips and silver wings
and i write about myself as if i'm the contents
of a vacuum cleaner

## GLITCHING

fairy lights clatter as tape unsticks
pieces of the wall give in like dead skin
and i wake up screaming because i'm being
attacked by crashing sounds
and creepy crawly strings of swarming bugs and
hard plastic
sweating and jumpy, tangled in pretty lights
sat upright in bed like a sad christmas tree
i look like a fool
and i feel the way cats do when we pick them up
except it's my own fault
because i put the damn lights up in the first place and
woke myself up at 3am when they gave up on me

now i'm not sure how to feel
or what to do
how do you just carry on
when your bedroom gives up on you

## OH WELL

i've never dated a guy who didn't leave me crying
on my birthday

# IF WE'RE ANYTHING AT ALL

he is a shipwreck on the south-east coast
and i am a magpie, scouring the earth endlessly
i pass him by every now and then
and he is vaguely familiar
but i feel nothing

he is splintering, rotting
giving parts of himself to the ocean day by day
forgetting what it was like to be loved
i am loving loving loving
everything i touch
it's never enough
beady eyes flickering, hunting, insatiable
always wondering 'is that it?'
stealing gold from every house i leave unsatisfied

he sheds flakes of paint, traces of me that never left
watches them drift away
feels a little colder each time
some days i'll drop a feather onto the beach
as i soar past
wonder if he'll ever find it
if he'll ever feel me again
how he'd savour me like his last breath
how big i would feel
but i know
i know it's not fair
and i have to leave him alone
i know that.

## A GIRL IS A SHAPESHIFTER

you'll see the gap between my thighs
but only when i part them for you

you'll find my ribs if you keep digging
between the seats in your car

where you dug hard into my sweet spots
roughed me up to see me weak

shrunk me till i was only bone
and bone and breast

eyelashes curl out of me, black like legs
of beetles crawling from my sockets

lipstick sticks in the cracks of my lips
the lady paints my head until i'm golden

my ivory skin reminds you of the skeleton at school
the one you can move and mock

and all it does is dangle there in front of you
accepting and smiling

you wish i'd smile more when i come
but i take my orgasms seriously

when people jump with parachutes
no one tells them to keep their hair in place

can't i just let the rush take over?
can't i forget myself for a moment?

i'm a sad excuse for a girl
always have been

and i like it that way
'pretty' is a stupid game

but i'll dress up for you
i'll be a doll for you

because i know how to find myself again
i've been changing who i am my whole life

a girl is a shapeshifter
and she shouldn't waste it on you

but she will
i will

i'll make myself brand-new for you
and i'll do it again once you're gone

and you'll kiss my ghost goodnight
when i leave her behind for you

and my real life goes on.

## MALUM IN SĒ

this heart was yours
before i swallowed it whole
the sun was fine
before i turned it all cold

and now what should i do
with the trees that sway?
should i dance along with them
or burn them away?

if it's music you want
i can snap all the bones
and if no one is listening
i'll do it alone

all the birds in the sky
they're so pretty it hurts
i will shoot them all down
watch them rot in the dirt

are you sure you can't stay?
i could clean up the blood
if i made the house perfect,
would it be enough?

i can still smell the flesh
through the damp wooden floor
i'll mop up the decay
or perhaps you'd like more?

we can swim in the waters
of all of my prey
dive in through the chimney
forget how to escape

this whole house can be flooded
your lungs filled with stones
we can drift down all heavy
i won't die alone

we can drown on the staircase
with pictures in frames
though we'll never come back
i'll remember your face

i'm not crazy i swear
i'm just lonely as hell
and i'm hoping that maybe
you're lonely as well

if you give me some love
i will let this bird fly
she can keep both her legs
and i won't let her die

but if i sleep alone,
and if you do me wrong,
this whole forest will burn.
there will be no more songs.

## HARMLESS KISSES TURN TO DAGGERS

red lips
dragged across shoulders
and spine
every inch of skin they can reach
so that when you go home to your wife
and she asks where i touched you
the map will be drawn out and ready for her

now i have no proof that you have a wife at all
but i see the way you shield your phone
i hear your speeches
about how you're 'not really a social media guy'
i've heard it before
and i found your facebook

i'll know the truth
when you never text me back
our conversation permanently ends on
*me: 'was nice seeing u last night x'*
days will pass
i'll go stale
bowing my head
learning to accept what you did
what i did
mourning not what we had
but what we destroyed
i was merely a hazel cat-eyed affair
she was your everything
until i tore it up
snapped your wedding ring like a haribo

i may be about to learn
that i destroyed someone's life
but at the very least i'll remind myself i tried
i did what i could to pass along the news
i left that lipstick as a warning sign
the outline of a crime scene

cheating men will learn
that lipstick—the traditional kind—
doesn't scrub off easily.
it doesn't flake away
revealing a seemingly untouched surface
a skin that never hurt a fly
no. it smudges. like grease.
leaves you with a permanent hue
of watered-down crimson
your entire body
blurred into flushed cheeks
burning hotter and hotter
as you scrub your skin from your bones
in a red panic
maybe then you will see
the shame you're meant to be feeling.

## CHURCHES

he tells me that if i walked into a church,
it would probably burst into flames.

this makes me laugh, because anyone
could burn down a building if they wanted to

and aren't we all deliberately not setting fires
every time we pull air into our chests?

now he's got me writing god into my poems
afraid he thinks of me as some empty thing

emptier than the church in this cold atheist chest
i sort of wish he'd worship me instead

god, if you sent him to me, i should tell you
my room's been full of smoke since he left

i should probably warn you, now he's gone,
he'll be looking for new things

to take in his arms and burn.

## THE DAY AFTER YOU BLOCKED ME

he asks me, 'do you like that?'
and i take a moment to try and figure out
which part of me he is touching

is he really so feather-soft
that he can fuck me without me noticing?
so gentle he may as well
have sent his ghost instead?
or is it just that sex with someone who isn't you
feels emptier then sleeping alone?

he asks me if he made me cum
and i say yes
because if he doesn't stop the atrocities
he's performing on my sacred body,
i think i might be sick

i tell him i can't do this
and he smears his dead fish lips across my mouth
but somehow it doesn't change my mind
somehow i cannot be enticed

i've decided to never have sex again

## THE LIFE OF A CANDLE

she woke me up at 9pm
and said 'you've got to see this'
i blinked my tired wick as it came to life
ready for the show
i've only got a couple more of these left
in my short lifetime
but she's done her best to savour me
to make me last
and to only light me on nights as magical
as this one.

he's the same guy as last time
and i think she's really into him
it's a shame i won't be here to see
if he sticks around
i won't be here to flicker in the playful dark
when she's bringing man after man
to try and forget the one she really wanted
begging each of them to fuck the sad out of her
i won't be here to watch them try
to laugh with her when they fail
and to help her settle into the quiet
when she finally realises
she's better off alone

## WHAT DO YOU THINK ABOUT AT NIGHT?

someone somewhere
is pointing a blade in my direction
they may be miles away,
across oceans,
buildings and mountains between us,
but i can feel it
paranoia doesn't need a map
it works with the unknown
and the unknown is something
i will never escape

## WAYS I'VE IMAGINED MY DEATH

i die sunbathing.
my warm skin spilled out across thriving grass,
sunglasses positioned just right,
i feel glorious
and i feel alive.
a man holds a brick above my head, ready to let go.
i open my eyes and he isn't there.

i die falling asleep.
sheets tangled between toes,
fan blowing soft against one leg,
loud buzzing in my ear.
the bee isn't a bee—it's a hornet. it's 2 feet long
and bright blue, and it's not here yet—he is miles
away, and his angry buzzing, his journey to my
deathbed, it's only just started.
i open the window and let the bee go.
i sleep with one eye open for the hornet, but he never
appears.

i die on your twitter feed.
clawing at the words, eyes glued to glowing screen,
reading the words 'worst day ever', and the next
tweet will read
'she was the light and now i can't see.
i can't believe i let her go. i can't believe it'
but the next tweet reads 'ffs arsenal' and i lay my
phone down beside my bed.
it's only the football and i don't die.

i die of an unknown allergic reaction.
tasting something new to erase the taste of your
mouth, your name, your famous cocktails. tongue
turns fuzzy at the unfamiliar. mind turns angry that i
lived 22 years without trying everything i could get
my hands on. some foods taste vile but they all taste
like being alive.
my tongue runs along my teeth and it can't find you
anymore.
i keep eating and i don't die, but you do.

## THE SLEEPLESS HOUSE

a boy cries himself to sleep,
only to wake up again and again.

a girl chats to her online boyfriend,
10 years older than her,
in a country she's never visited.
they will never meet.

their mother is pacing in the kitchen,
contemplating pills.
she has a big day tomorrow and she needs rest,
but what if someone needs her in the night?
what if the sleep swallows her
and she can't drive her child to the hospital?

their father lives with someone else now,
but the sleepless house still gets to him.
he's watching a new city from his lover's balcony.
nothing ever happens, but he likes to think
he makes the streets feel safe.

their father's lover sleeps soundly.
his job eats him alive in daylight,
but night is not a threat to him.
he wishes his love could let go a little.
they'd both sleep better side by side.

back at the sleepless house,
the family cat has got business to take care of.
she follows her usual routine of covering her tracks
and she disappears into the fog.
they mustn't know where she is going.
she'll never let them see.

## ANIMAL PLAY

when i was a child, i used to bite people.
i mean, really bite them.
so hard that my top and bottom teeth could almost
touch with someone's skin between them.

and they would cry.
they'd weaken like the branches on trees
we were too heavy to swing from
like sandcastles crumbling beneath feet

and whatever they were doing before
that made me so uncomfortable i felt the need to hurt
them, well, they stopped. immediately.

i've always known violence is not the answer,
but sometimes when a boy pins you down
and you see satisfaction in his crinkled nose
while he winds you and strangles you
and tells you he's the boss
you'll find that violence
is the only thing he'll understand.

it reached a point where i'd bite someone
and i'd tell them to stop being silly
when they started to cry
because i knew the limits of my jaw
and i thought i could choose whether to give
a warning bite or an attacking bite
but some stupid kids would cry anyway
as soon as they felt teeth press their skin.

i grew older, and generally, the violence settled.
as a teenager, i rarely had to bite anyone.
i did, however, begin growing my nails out.
one day a boy, a good friend of mine, thought it was
funny to tighten his hand around my throat.
i dug my nails into his wrist until he couldn't hold on
any longer.
he left the room, only to return minutes later to show
me his bleeding arm.
'look what you did!' he said bitterly. i just smiled
and shrugged because he chose this.

from age 14 to 18, whenever a boy decided
he'd like to play rough with me,
you'd hear a voice from one corner or another
shouting 'be careful, she bites! she claws! that girl's
a savage animal!'

and i loved being that girl.
the girl who earned the respect of the toughest boys
by breaking their egos down until they couldn't
look me in the eye.

i loved that they could never pin me down
to try and kiss me
because if someone was going to kiss me
they didn't want to look like a predator
and they didn't want to leave the kiss with injuries.

i loved that when i finally let a boy get close enough,
our hands rested on each other gently
and our mouths were nothing but soft.

## UNTANGLED

you'll know it's really over
when he smiles at a girl miles away
and you don't feel it;
nothing pulls in your chest.
your soul doesn't know what his is up to.

you'll know the ties have been cut
when you realise you're on bad terms
and it's a shame, you suppose
but it doesn't feel terrible.
it doesn't really feel like anything.

you were always meant to hate each other.
remember how you used to claw and scream

how you'd use friendly debate as an excuse
to tell him he was wrong about everything

how one morning when you woke up,
he said 'you kept shoving me in your sleep'

how when one of you opened up about a passion,
the other would throw back a judgemental
*'really?'*

and maybe it was fun playing tug of war,
but it's hard to play when there's nothing left
to hold onto.
nothing left to be said that could pull
on your chest until it hurts.

you've untangled from him now,
free to go anywhere you like,
do as you please without him shattering,
fall asleep without his heartbeat
ringing in your ears

and it's good.
you're free, and it feels good.

but sometimes it's hard to feel important
when you kiss a stranger
and nobody breaks.

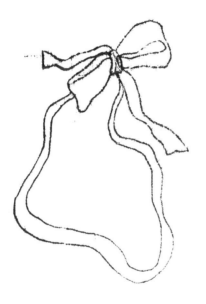

## GIRLS GROW OUT OF PLAYING WITH DOLLS AND MEN GROW INTO IT

cut-out pieces of oiled-up bodies
newsprint pornstars stuck to my mirror
gleaming teeth and pricked-up brows
women who are fierce and confident
all in the name of male approval

women who are a little bit wild
little bit naïve
little bit ready to throw everything away
for a man they're not even attracted to

that's the dream
and a man's dream becomes a little girl's dream
as soon as she realises her dreams don't matter

what i'd have given for a chubby older man
with nothing to his name
to tell me i was special

to know how lucky i had made someone
being a gift they never earned, a blessing
so worth holding onto
they'd remind me every day
how utterly perfect i was

but little girls grow up
and when they get big
towering over little thoughts
little beliefs
little things that used to matter

they can see
from way up here
the dreams they let go at 11 years old
when they thought they were a waste
dreams so big they never really left

and now that i am grown
i sleep with men twice as good looking as me
they take me as a blessing
and i never text them again
i rate them from 1 to 10 in a little book
and i move onto the next
never stopping long enough to let them keep me
to let them have anything more
than what i already gave them

because i know now
i know that i am special
i am the greatest gift i could possibly give
and i am mine

he will go home and get back on the app
desperately searching for something beautiful
obedient
loyal

something he will eventually realise is a sex doll
who he will invest in during a midlife crisis
and name after me
or after another girl who was prettier
or gave better head
or laughed at his jokes about the working class
whatever

we all have oceans and moons
paying tribute to our chests
so what does it matter whose voice
he installs into his adult bath toy?

those hopeless men
we've blocked all their numbers
and we can't hear them from the tops
of our prince-less castles
we don't remember the silly things
they used to demand from us
when we thought our only place
was beneath them

everything i do now
it's all for me
and i will never stop
looking for more.

## I LOVE IT

'you love it', he says smugly
while nailing my body into the wall
like a poster he's a little too eager to hang up.
i respond with some jolted words, if 'uh huh' counts
as words, and he bangs harder

what dimension is he trying to send me to?
why is he so desperately and angrily trying to shove
me out of this one?

i used to think having someone inside me would
make me feel close, connected, like i'm a part of
something
i do realise that my being here is a pretty key part in
the event, but i feel like i'm somehow getting in his
way

he's still banging and i feel as if i might go all the
way through the wall into the neighbour's house

'you love it', he repeats
and i smile the same fake smile that made him say
'there's that smile' the last time i had to pretend he
was making me happy

i'm not sure why i do it, really
why i pretend to be happy to make other people
happy
you'd think this guy would have other things to feel
proud of
but i'm sort of convinced this is it

this clunky mashing of skin, sweat pouring off of
him and onto me, hair getting stuck to everything,
his greatest achievement

i want him to feel good about himself, like he has a
purpose, but i'm running out of patience
starting to doubt that giving him purpose is my job in
the first place

running the risk of ruining his testosterone fest,
when he tells me i love it for the third time,
i respond, 'do i really, though?'

## ERROR 402

the dating app tells me, for the 4th time,
'this isn't gonna work out.'

'why?' i ask, picking at the stitches
where my online persona has been pulled out.

they look me up and down,
pondering the body they know so well
oh, how they wish they never met me.

exhaling a hot computer fan breath,
they say, 'we are not a doctor,
we are not a church;
we are not here to fix your heart.'

i tell them i never expected them to.
that all i ever asked was
'fuck me till the sad is gone'
and they pull up the evidence:

every message i've sent
to a man who i wasn't meant to love
asking 'why don't you care about me?'
the men say 'i thought you just wanted to fuck'

they say
'you can't post a picture
of yourself naked in the woods
and expect people to fall in love.
you just can't.'

and i say 'yes i can—
fuck off!'
although my confidence is wavering.

they say,
'ERROR 402
your account has been banned
for violating the community guidelines.'

## INSOMNIAC MEETS SOMETHING RESTFUL

he and i used to keep each other up
with our rattling bones
but you
are one of those maniacs who just decides when to
sleep and actually does it without even trying
i keep looking for reasons to stay awake
things to worry about
limbs that can't stay still
but this time they're all mine
and i keep getting sucked into this functional sleep
of yours
i keep letting go without tossing and turning
and i'm not sure how to handle it

## SWALLOW THE NIGHT

don't we all dream in tangerine?
lilo floating into the sun
it doesn't burn, just tickles
underwater galaxies
singing along to killer queen
painting clouds and swallowing guns
holding hearts between our teeth

dandelions giggle
granting wishes between fingers
we undress them drinking lemonade
whispering names of crushes
he tries on your heart-shaped glasses
the sky's so white you can't stand it

pouring stardust into cocktails
taste of space on his sea salt skin
everything is cannibalism
you squeeze my hand when the mermaid
starts to cry
his fingers are too hot for her skin
and the birds give us directions in english
he barbecues sweet peppers on the edge of the sun
and the sun says you can't stay here
what if someone sees
the moon says 'what the hell do you think you're
doing?'
and you pick shards of jupiter out of your teeth
'i think i'd like to wake up now,'
you whisper to me
'i think i'm ready to go home.'

## NEW THROWS OLD INTO A BLACK HOLE

i can't teach him your repetition, how you kissed my
cheeks like a fire alarm running on fresh
batteries, but he brings me a calm i never knew
existed. i don't have to teach him anything. the ways
he's nothing like you are the best things
about him.

## THE BALCONY I

i like it when you let half of me go
hanging off the balcony
you hold me steady at the hip like a paperweight

i like how, up here, we're in the sky
how it surrounds not only our heads but our feet
bare and red on the cold metal grid

i like how you push me into any corner you can find
how it doesn't matter if it's my bedroom walls or a
feeble frame hanging in the air

you will hold me tightly in the corner
and i will be safe and sound
you make the world disappear every time

i don't think the balcony has any idea
that before us,
it was just a fire escape

before you,
these steps were here
so i could get away

but as long as your hands are on my neck
and your lips are on my skin,
i'm not going anywhere

as long as you're here,
i have nothing
to run from.

## THE BALCONY II

bend me over the balcony as we kiss
let my head drop back and then catch it
tell me i could be afraid of heights, or i could not
cup my face like a baby bird and say
'so choose. are you afraid?'
and you know i'll say no. not anymore.

bend me over the balcony and follow me.
we'll leave a mark on the map wherever we land.

bend me over the balcony and fuck me like
everyone's watching. or like nobody in the world can
see us and we're far too distant for the city lights to
catch us. nobody will ever catch us.

bend me over the balcony until i fall, but not really,
just shake me and say you're only kidding. wrap me
tightly in your arms and laugh as i freak out because
'i could've died, you dick!'

bend me over the balcony until i say please.
please pull me up. please just take me right here.
please stay the night.

bend me over the balcony so that when you leave
because you'd never stay the night, i can feel you in
my rust-splintered spine, my aching shoulders, my
tender neck.

leave me with something colder and dirtier than you,
but something that is still worth writing about.

## IF WE HAD GROWN UP TOGETHER

my mother keeps all of my milk teeth in a little jar
sometimes i knock it over to watch my youth
scatter like rattling snow that refuses to fade
sometimes i wish the memories would go away

one time i told you to hold out your hands
and i tipped the jar upside down
you weren't sure what to say
with a fragile handful of my teeth
as i watched curiously
they still chatter just the same

i always say,
if we'd known each other when we were 5,
we would've fallen in love
we didn't meet at the right time

no, it has always been our time
and we could've loved earlier

we could've spent more summers together
god, my childhood would have been so full
so bright and so loud

i can see us skipping with bandaged knees
holding sticky hands
knotted hair bouncing along with the clouds

did you learn my first words
when you felt the weight of my mouth?

did you hear us dancing
so clumsy we fall

saved by the creaking of the trampoline
sky ready to catch us if we jump too high

our heads hanging over the bath side by side
as our mothers cut gum out of our hair

did you see us?
did you see us growing up?

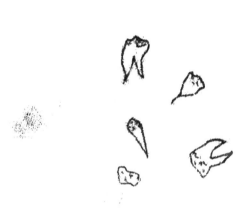

## THE SUN AND SOMETHING ELSE

your chest rises and falls against my back
heartbeat rumbles like wild horses
did you know
your chest could claim the ocean
and god would just let it happen
god would ask, 'can i get you anything else?'

my mouth is the chimney
of a house father christmas steers clear of
the smoke all comes out black
the bricks weep ever so quietly

your milky way fingers have felt everything
but they're still heavenly soft
still strawberries and cream
your touch turns me into a better thing

my skin is the ground of a cemetery
after the dead have awoken
and clawed their way out
leaving me broken
they couldn't bear to stay down there
most days i can't either

you are the sun
and it would be easier to write about us
if i were the moon
but i am not a pretty light
i am not a thing that glows

you slide off my dress
like summer pulls ice cream from cones
and i try not to stain your skin
with my charcoal body
my crumbling lips
they crack right open when i smile
when you tell me i'm pretty
and god can bear to look at me
because i don't look so bad through your eyes

my happy bleeding mouth stains the carpet
paints my fingers metallic
but you don't say a word
because you're daylight and you know
that light can be blinding
and if i'm going to be happy
if i'm going to get better
at first,
it's going to hurt

## YES

my body flinches against his touch, and he says
sorry. he shifts away, dividing us like we're two
separate things.
i need space sometimes and he gets it.

his hands contemplate before reaching for my waist;
just a sweet moment, just a taste; he wants a little bit
of me. i roll away, giggling, and he says 'okay, okay.'
his hands raised in surrender,
accepting my rejection.
'i'm kidding, god,' i say.
'aren't you gonna fight for me?'

he grips my hips too tight and i let out, 'wait… wait,
that hurts.' i never use the word 'no.' i never have
to. he chuckles, admits he got carried away, and he
holds me soft until i call the shots. until i decide i
want more.

and just like that, i know what consent means.
just like that, i'll never expect him to fight for me.
how is it that i had to learn from him that men
shouldn't treat women's bodies like battle grounds?
how selfishly i wished
that my hips would start wars
once weapons are drawn, it's not a game anymore
how is it that he had to teach me this?
how is it that i didn't know how to draw my own
lines, to create my own boundaries, until he asked if
his kisses were okay and didn't rush me to say 'yes'?

## A VOW

on the days we don't leave the house,
i love you to the fridge and back

## SAFE

you walk me backwards through the house
and my toes try to scan the floor before we reach it
for pins i've never used
and messes i tidied before you got here
i try to turn my head, check behind me for safety,
and you pull my face back to yours, saying
'trust me'

my face in your hands
your nose kissing mine
i trust you

remember the first time we met
i let you hold my wrists above my head
the first time we kissed

remember how i giggled
how i held so still
because you were already the kindest man
i'd ever allowed to lock me out
of the control room
you always knew you were
pressing the right buttons
but you kept your eyes on my face anyway
you made sure i was happy anyway

and now we creep gently across the carpet
you guide me like a child
and i tread softly, blindly
across the balancing beam of the living room

you're the only one who knows how to make me
question
where i am in my own home
the only one who can keep me on my toes
while they feel their way across familiar ground

all the while you know what's ahead
you can see exactly where we're going
but still, you're looking at me instead

## I HAD A DREAM ABOUT US

i press chamomile flowers on your tongue
the moon on the carpet is quite fitting
absorbing dreams like gone-off milk
the sun sets
us up on a date
and we kill its family

yellow powder on the roof of your mouth
the hole in the sky is quite concerning
absorbing stars like we breathe sleep
the sun sets
and we die

## THE ENDING I HOPE FOR

he lays his skull heavy across my ribs
and i feel the same sort of trust
that you feel as a child on the beach
being buried in stones by a loved one
and knowing they will dig you back up again
a kind of weight that is strange
yet comforting
pressing yet relieving
and i hope he never moves
i hope we lay like this,
skeletons interlinked,
fingers hooked together,
skull buried inside my chest
i hope we lay like this until we're gone
i hope when they find our hollow bones,
his skull is beneath my rib cage
sitting where my heart once was
because when we're gone
when we've decayed
and my heart is no longer there
i still want him in it

## TANTRUM

his replies are getting blunter
and i'd like to rip my skin off
and throw it at him
to perhaps get a little more attention

## HUNTER

trickle down my thigh like your work is done
the mess we made will spread as you drip
off of me and onto the floor

and we'll just watch because we're tired
and we're fulfilled and we don't care
i'll just buy a new carpet

tell me i'm not like other girls
other girls don't let you do the things i do
tell me you'll text
and then don't

crawl out of my bed like a cat who's got
hunting to do
disappear into the night and see if i care
(i do)

smile at your phone when i give in and text first
but don't actually smile
just do it in my head when i pretend you're still
interested

ignore my text and resume fucking her
and telling her she's not like other girls

tell her you like her so much
because she's nothing like me

## HUMMINGBIRD

the night we met
i swear i swallowed a hummingbird whole
my chest buzzed till i was dizzy
and now i stay in bed just to be safe
from falling over without your arms to catch me

the night you left
it hurt the same way that kissing you always hurt
so good i can't stand it
so tragic i can't stand it
sometimes it's not that i feel nothing—
it's that i feel so much that i can't tell my fingers
from my toes
because they all tingle so loud i start to lose them
i can't tell love from hate
because they're both so fuzzy
and falling feels like flying

kisses = good
leaving = bad
i'll try to remember that
but it's hard when my chest flutters just the same
as the day you fed me stardust
and told me to whisper your name
instead i giggled for hours
god i loved how my belly ached

i know you broke me
i know we said goodbye
and maybe i'll start to process that
once this damn bird dies

# A LETTER TO THE BOY WHO LEFT HER

i can tell when she's thinking about you
because her face goes tired and her words blur out of
focus
dilute until she washes away
she's been losing a lot of sleep lately.
i'm surprised by the way she still mentions you
when pink floyd comes on
or we see a picture of someone we all knew
together
or a guy wearing the same shoes you used to have
she looks for you everywhere
feels victory when she finds you
as if eating your favourite foods somehow brings
you back to her

she still writes about you.
can you believe there's any 'you' left in her?
that you made so many things light up in her chest
that two years later
she's still trying to flush you out with the rain
which i'm pretty sure is full of you, too

i don't know the story like she does.
i know you loved the way she said 'kiss me'
and you said you could tell her anything
and you told her you don't like labels.
i know she said she doesn't either,
and she insists that's the truth, but i'm telling you,
it isn't.
her face spills so many aches
she doesn't have to tell me

that you were always half-way out the door,
and she needed you to be in or out
because she felt unsafe with it left wide open.
but she knew the only way she could keep you
was to barely have you at all

it wasn't much, but it was enough.
it was enough that you told her she was pretty that
one time
and when it got to the end,
it was enough that you said,
'we'll see what happens.'
so, she waited. and she cried into my lap,
and she asked all your friends what was going on
and they said 'nothing.'
but you left her with something
and that something is still here after all this time.

she hasn't said your name in her sleep for two
months, and i'm beginning to think that the lights
have gone.
maybe you have finally left.
what i ask of you, please, no matter how bored you
get...

don't come back.

don't come back.

# THOUGHTS OF HIS EYES AFTER HE DUMPS YOU

blue eyes as oceans, but also as bruises. as icing with
artificial colouring. limp bodies, cold, still hoping
but no longer hopeful. blue as this is what you're left
with when you swallow the sky.

brown eyes as chocolate, but also as rust. a fireplace
that comforts in a house you don't belong in.
glistening horses on race tracks. they leave so fast
but you don't forget.

green eyes as forests, but also as loneliness. new life
growing in corners we've left untouched.
whispers in the morning. apologies: i didn't plan
this. green as he was always meant to leave so you
could grow.

grey eyes as silver, but also as fading hair. as you're
not supposed to see him like this. as he's always
known too much. grey squirrels kill the red ones.
grey glistens on black roads when the rain throws us
off track. grey as the smoke of the crash.

hazel eyes as there are places that aren't made of
him, and you will find them.

## SPACES

the night you begged me to take you back
and i said i'd sleep on it,
i lay basking in the cool space surrounding me
the feeling of utter bliss from sleeping alone
finally found me
after all those nights where i thought i needed you
with me to feel at peace.

when i dreamt of you laying by my side,
and the possibility that this could be
my last night away from you,
my heartbeat shook me awake at 4am.

and that's how i knew
we did the right thing
when we ended it.

## SOMETIMES WE FORGET

don't you see how the air keeps letting you have it?
how the breeze can't help but touch your face?
don't you see that you're wanted?

## LONDON

london,
the stench of sewage seeps from your clogged pores
but i love you anyway.
maybe it's the way you can still breathe through all
this smoke, the way your sky is still blue despite us
and how we try so hard to fill you with grey.

your blood runs murky through the thames and we
will never know how many bodies your veins have
swallowed, but somehow it doesn't matter what's
in that river. somehow the tourists still gaze into it,
exclaiming 'how beautiful.'

london doesn't greet you the way the countryside
does.
the passing dog walkers don't say good morning,
and wide-open spaces aren't waiting to be touched.
london has already been touched. it has already been
loved.
when a farm girl steps out of liverpool street
station, she steps into london's mouth and she lets it
swallow her.
there's so much happening down here, so much light
and so much dark and what is that smell? look at the
size of that burger—where can i get one of those?
everything is everywhere and her senses are
crowded but at least they're not empty.

nothing in london is ever empty.

## SOME KIND OF SELF-CARE

i used to fill my mouth with coconut oil
after every cigarette
because i read online that it would draw out the
toxins

i used to plaster my greying skin with every
concoction that nobody had heard of
each of them with their own claims
that they would make my face brand-new

stuffed my mouth with almonds and berries
drank water until i couldn't move
put kale in all of my smoothies and told myself
that it didn't taste like dirt

i thought i did everything
to fix my broken body
i thought i was taking care of myself

now i eat what i want
i go outside for the right kind of air
and i can't go near coconut oil without smelling
smoke
i don't have rituals
i don't throw money at every rare plant i can find
i don't 'swear by' products that are illustrated with
hollow promises

i don't smoke anymore
and it turns out
that's all my body was begging for

## HOW I'LL REMEMBER THIS ROOM

i. the door

he always locked it.
i always forgot.
we kept quiet on one side
and set fires on the other.
it never slammed in october.

ii. the desk

that's where he laid his jacket.
his ever-buzzing phone.
his identity to the rest of the world.
he left his family, his friends
and his job, all on the desk.
stacks of paperwork and texts
and 'are you with that girl again?'
that can wait until later.

iii. the bed

we broke it the night we met.
it never stopped trying, though.

## GIRLHOOD/BOYHOOD

i'm picking gravel out of grazed knees
blood blackening under ragged fingernails
i wipe my hands on baggy jeans
get up and resume running
chasing or being chased
i don't recall which one
later,
a boy gives me a nipple cripple
laughing because it hurts more on girls
i'm laughing too because i'm 9 years old
my knee sends blinding pain into his crotch
he begins to cry and now the game is over
i tell him i'm sorry i went too far
i carry him until we find an adult, his long curls
sticking to damp cheeks
and we don't hurt each other again
until 7 years later.

in the meantime, i was one of the boys
following my brother and his friends around, first to
die in every game, fastest tree climber, best at holding back tears
until i became one of the girls, painting everyone's
nails pretty but never as pretty as mine, painting over
my skin, painting painting won't stop painting until
everything is pretty, but people still laughed at me
so i plucked my eyebrows until they were no longer
mine, pulled on my hair *'why won't you grow'* until
it fell out and never came back, scratching hard at
the spots on my skin, leaving dents that will never
fill in

the girls broke me
and when i finally turned back to the boys
they wouldn't take me
with this skin, this hair
these eyebrows, that had gone from thick to thin
while beauty standards had done the opposite
so i kept changing changing
learning how to be someone that matters

the boy says sorry
when he touches things that have never been touched
and i flinch under his calloused fingers.
he finds peace in the curve of my hip,
the parts of me that are okay without trying,
his fingers know where the soft bits are
and i learn that my body is fine
it has always been fine

the boys made me tough
made me funny
made the girls afraid of me

the girls made me stop fighting
made me pretty
didn't get me
'you can't joke about stuff like that. you just can't.'

but we were just kids back then
pushing and pulling
testing the limits
learning the words
making a mess

somewhere along the lines, we figured out the truth
that we're not born tough
born pretty
born anything

the hardest part for all of us
was figuring out who we are
when the grown-ups stopped watching
when they felt their work was done
suddenly labels start to dissolve
no more 'violent boy'
'bitchy girl'
suddenly those things are gone
no more shifting the blame onto stereotypes
that we once grew into
that we've now learned to escape from

and it's just you now
no more girl, no more boy
only your name and your voice

and who knows
what the hell we've done with it all.

## A PICTURE OF SELF IN SPRINGTIME

who is she?

sitting with a yellow notebook
beneath yellow flowers
they bloom right over her head this time of year
and no one
will ever find her here

she's not alone:
she shares her hideout with the bumble bees
they buzz all around her,
not minding that she is there
(although they got there first)

she trusted the sky today
to stay warm long enough and let her write
between the tall, swaying stalks that still see her as a
child

she doesn't always know what to say
but that's all right, according to the soft
sunshine-coloured petals that tickle her nose
every time she raises her head hopelessly
wondering where the words are, if they even exist

sometimes she's a woman
22 years along
a song that you'll try to forget
a part of your story worth holding onto
if you'd like to avoid plot holes

she's her mother's
'what the hell do you think you're doing'
and her father's
'well i don't bloody know do i'
she's the note that spoils the rhythm
because she knows it's the only way to get noticed

maybe she's fingernails, frantically tapping
on any surface they can find
pulled-out eyelashes in a neat little pile
tea leaves scattered over every counter

but right now
she is a girl breathing quietly
through spring's blossoming organs
watching flowers open their tiny mouths to yawn
hiding from the footsteps on the nearby path
and whispering to the field,
'i'm sorry i woke you'

## ABOUT THE AUTHOR

Jasmine S. Higgins is a writer and art student living in London. She self-published her debut poetry
collection *A Girl Is A Shapeshifter* in 2019 and is
currently working on her first novel that will hope-
fully get finished at some point before she dies.
She's 22 and intends to stay that way.

Printed in Great Britain
by Amazon